CLASSICAL HISTORIAN
American Civics

American Songs: Patriotic, Folk, Fun & End of the Trail

Book 7
K-5 Workbook

BY JOHN DE GREE
CLASSICAL HISTORIAN

Copyright © 2024 by Classical Historian™ All Rights Reserved.
Published by Classical Historian™
Printed in the United States of America.
Revised Edition.

No part of this book may be used or reproduced in any manner whatsoever without written permission except in the case of a brief quotation embodied in critical articles and reviews.
Graphic Artist: Patty Roberts

More Information: john@classicalhistorian.com
www.classicalhistorian.com

Classical Historian American Civics
Elementary Curriculum

Book One
Introduction

Part 1
Law and Morality

Part 2
Ancient, Medieval, and Modern Heritage

Part 3
Founding of the United States of America

Book Two
Limited Government and the Three Branches

Part 1
Three Branches of Government

Part 2
The Executive Branch

Part 3
The Judicial Branch

Part 4
The Legislative Branch

Book Three
The Bill of Rights and Amendments

Part 1
Bill of Rights and Amendments 1-5

Part 2
Amendments 6-10

Part 3
Amendments

Continued on next page

ELEMENTARY CURRICULUM
Continued

BOOK FOUR
HOW A LAW IS MADE

Part 1
How a Law is Made

Part 2
Heroes and Virtues

BOOK FIVE
AMERICAN REFORMS

Part 1
Slavery

Part 2
Civil Rights

BOOK SIX
PATRIOTISM

Part 1
Important Documents

Part 2
Timeline

Part 3
Folk Tales

BOOK SEVEN
AMERICAN SONGS

Part 1
Patriotic

Part 2
Folk

Part 3
Fun

Part 4
End of the Trail

Introduction

The American educational system has been in crisis for generations. Aside from the catastrophic academic failure of many of our schools, American students graduate high school and college without an understanding and appreciation of civics. Civics is the study of the duties and rights of a citizen, and in a republic, part of that study is an education in virtue. In a free republic, it is necessary for self-governing citizens to not only understand but also appreciate and have a patriotic love of their country.

In many American schools, teachers instruct students to hate their own country, its founders, and its history. For the most part, though, students remain ignorant of the meaning of the United States of America. If citizens of a free republic do not understand their own rights and government, that country will not remain free. As John Adams wrote, "Knowledge will forever govern ignorance; and a people who mean to be their own governors must arm themselves with the power which knowledge gives."

American Civics fills the great void in American education. It is an engaging and age-appropriate *American Civics* curriculum for elementary and junior high school students. It teaches America's ancient and medieval heritage, the great story of its founding, the Constitution, and how the American government works, including the rights and duties of citizens. But more than this, *American Civics* instructs children in the virtues citizens need to self-govern in a republic.

On July 4, 1924, in a speech to the National Education Association, President Calvin Coolidge said, "It needed but little contemplation to determine that the greatest obstacle to freedom was ignorance. If there was to be self-government, if there was to be popular sovereignty, if there was to be an almost unlimited privilege to vote and hold office, if the people were going to maintain themselves and administer their own political and social affairs, it was necessary as a purely practical matter that they should have a sufficiently trained and enlightened intelligence to accomplish that end. Popular government could only be predicated on popular education."

Most American educators are no longer engaged in the teaching of civics and training young minds about the freedoms citizens enjoy in a free republic. There is little or no training in the universal concept of virtue, which is moral excellence required of free citizens. Join us at Classical Historian to teach *American Civics* to America's youth and equip our youth to be active citizens to keep our republic free.

Ideas for Instruction

American Civics is written with the idea that before a student enters the 6th grade, he will have learned all the materials that are in the seven civics books. We begin with perhaps one of the most important books, Book Seven.

I. Using Songs to Teach Patriotism with *Book Seven*

Singing is an effective way to build patriotism in children, to teach vocabulary, and to foster belonging and friendship. In fact, when the Communist Soviet Union controlled many countries in the twentieth century, they banned singing of national patriotic songs in those nations they controlled. Communists attempted to kill children's love of country so they could be manipulated easier. When children have no emotional attachment to their own country, they will not grow up loving and appreciating their homeland. In today's America, children and adults have little if no knowledge of our common musical heritage. Classical Historian aims to change this. **Book Seven contains songs and guitar chords.**

American Civics songs are found on Spotify, YouTube Music Channel, Apple Music, iTunes, Deezer, and Our YouTube Channel at this link: *https://distrokid.com/hyperfollow/classicalhistorian/american-civics*

When driving with your children or at home, simply play the songs. Very soon, your children will have all the songs memorized and will be singing along. If someone in your family or in your co-op can play the guitar, have sing-along get-togethers with the guitar. Your children will learn to love America's songs and our country.

Using Songs in the Classroom with Book Seven

There are many ways to use these songs in the classroom:

- **A. Transition:** Have students sing the song as they transition from subject to subject. Set the expectation that every student sings and is ready to go for the next subject when the song is finished.
- **B. Clean-Up:** Train students to understand that a particular song is the "clean-up song," and set the expectation that every student sings along and is done cleaning up by the end of the song.
- **C. Movement Break:** Have students come up with hand motions for the songs and sing and move to provide a break in between lessons.
- **D. Game:** Play basic memory games with the lyrics. For example, arrange students in a circle and have each student say the next word in the song. The student who says the wrong word is out. The last student remaining is the winner.

II. Activities for American Civics Books One through Six

Lower Elementary (K-2nd Grade)

A. Read-aloud: The teacher can read out loud the lesson to the students as they follow the words in the book, or a student can read out loud the lesson. Together, the teacher and student then answer the questions in complete sentences. The teacher writes the answers on the board and the students copy the sentences, paying attention to correct spelling and punctuation.

B. Coloring Pages: After reading out loud and answering the questions, students color the pages.

C. Videos: Students watch the videos to reinforce the lessons.

D. *Book Six* Timeline: Color the timeline cards, cut them out, place them in their correct spot, and practice lining the cards up in chronological order. Note: Only Book Six contains the timeline cards.

Middle Elementary (3rd Grade)

A. Read-aloud: Students read out loud the lessons.

B. Activity Page: Students write the answers on their own. As a class, the teacher and students review the answers.

C. Paraphrasing: Using the key words located in the back of each book, students rewrite the lessons on their own. Please see detailed explanation on the following pages.

D. *Book Six* Timeline: Color the timeline cards, cut them out, place them in their correct spot, and practice lining the cards up in chronological order. Note: Only *Book Six* contains the timeline cards. Please see a detailed explanation on the following pages.

E. Videos: Students watch the videos to reinforce the lessons. Please see a detailed explanation on the following pages.

Upper Elementary (4th-5th Grade)

A. Read-aloud: Students read out loud the lessons.

B. Activity Page: Students write the answers on their own. As a class, the teacher and students review the answers.

C. Paraphrasing: Using the key words located in the back of each book, students rewrite the lessons on their own. Please see a detailed explanation on the following pages.

D. Oral Presentation: Students commit their paraphrase to memory and make an oral presentation. Please see a detailed explanation on the following pages. Book Six Timeline: Cut out timeline cards and place them in their correct spot. Practice lining the cards up in chronological order.

E. *Book Six* Timeline: Color the timeline cards, cut them out, place them in their correct spot, and practice lining the cards up in chronological order. Note: Only Book Six contains the timeline cards.

F. Videos: Students watch the videos to reinforce the lessons.

III. Detailed Explanation of the Activities
Paraphrasing a Lesson Using Key Words

A very effective learning method is to rewrite lessons in one's own words. The rewriting process compels a student to think, analyze what is most important, organize, and create. Below is an excerpt from American Civics, Book One and an example of a rewrite. The key words to each lesson are located at the end of each book.

Lesson: "The American Revolution" from Book One

From 1775 to 1783, the United States of America fought Great Britain and won its independence. The war was called The American Revolution. Americans fought bravely during the war, and many sacrificed their lives. Americans did not want to be ruled by a king. They wanted to rule themselves. The war is called a revolution because Americans changed their government from a monarchy to a republic. In a monarchy, a king rules and has much power. A king is not voted into power. When a king dies, his oldest son becomes the next king. Americans overthrew the King of Great Britain and established a republic. In a republic, citizens vote for leaders and the leaders make the laws. Americans established the first republic in the modern world. At its founding, it was the freest country on Earth.

Key Words Found at the End of the Book:

1. The American Revolution 2. Monarchy 3. Republic 4. The United States of America

Rewrite by a Student:

The American Revolution was a war the United States of America fought against Great Britain from 1775 to 1783. In this war, Americans gained independence from Great Britain. Americans also overthrew the monarchy and established a republic. A **monarchy** is when a king rules, and when the king dies, his son becomes the ruler. A **republic** is where citizens vote for representatives and representatives make laws. **The United States of America** was the freest place on Earth when it was founded as the first republic in the modern world.

Oral Presentation

The oral presentation is an ideal educational tool for the teacher to help the student learn the materials and to teach the student how to speak in front of others. It is best if the student presents without notes, and if the student does not worry about memorizing the presentation word for word. To aid in this, the teacher should take an incremental approach, allowing the students some notes for the first talk, and then making the notes decrease for each talk until the student does not use any notes.

For the first talk, the teacher may instruct the student to use ten words as his notes. Then, for the second talk, eight, and so on, until the student is not using any notes. Students will practice until their presentation is successful.

Presentations should be done in front of as many people as possible. In addition to occurring during class time, presentations could take place during an academic showcase, where parents, grandparents, and whole families are invited. The more this can happen, the better the students will present and the more comfortable they will be speaking in front of others. It is also best if the teacher organizes a final presentation of the year, where students dress formally. To do this, the teacher should plan the event about two months in advance. Invitations should go out to the families, and students should know that this event is happening. Because the students know their families will attend, they will work extra hard to present well. In a case-by-case situation, the teacher can decide to allow a student or two to use notes during the presentation.

Timeline Cards in *Book Six*

In *Book Six*, there are ten key events in American History, with the event year and a short description. Each event has an accompanying image to color. Students memorize the dates and events and color the timeline cards. Then, students cut out the timeline cards and place them in the appropriate space. Students then practice placing timeline cards in chronological order on a table or flat surface. Students can store their cut-out timeline cards in a pouch in *Book Six*.

American Civics Animated Videos

Classical Historian Civics videos present the materials in an entertaining format while maintaining all educational value of the lessons. At the printing of this series, video lessons are still in production. Go to www.classicalhistorian.com for more information.

IV. Scope and Sequence for Teaching American Civics in an Elementary School or in a Co-op

In an in-person elementary school or co-op, we recommend the following books be taught in this order:

Kindergarten:	Books 1 and 2
First Grade:	Books 3 and 4
Second Grade:	Books 5 and 6
Third Grade:	Books 1 and 2: Oral Presentations
Fourth Grade:	Books 3 and 4: Oral Presentations
Fifth Grade:	Books 5 and 6: Oral Presentations

Each book has about 15 lessons. For a school year that lasts 32-26 weeks, students can learn about one lesson per week. We strongly recommend singing the songs in all grade levels, and as a school, throughout the year.

V. Scope and Sequence for Teaching all Seven Books in One School Year in the Home School

In a nine-month school year, if students learn two to three lessons per week, they will finish the complete curriculum before the end of the year. The books may be used with different-aged children, at the same time, or separately. The family may also teach the books over and over. A five-year-old would complete the curriculum, then again as a 3rd grader, and then again as a 5th grader. At each level, the child would learn at an age-appropriate level, and as the subject is government, repetition is needed to cement the material into the student's memory.

Closing

Civics is a topic that is often talked about as a subject Americans need to learn. The best age to start learning civics is at the youngest possible. Classical Historian is excited to add these materials in the hopes of teaching American kids about their country and the freedoms we enjoy. We aim to train young Americans to value our common American heritage, liberty, and to be ready to defend freedom when and where it is challenged.

John De Gree and Jessica De Gree

Table of Contents

I. Patriotic

The Pledge of Allegiance	2
The Star-Spangled Banner	4
America the Beautiful	6
Yankee Doodle	8
You're a Grand Old Flag	10
Battle Hymn of the Republic	12

II. Folk

Oh, Susana	16
Skip to my Lou	18
She'll be Coming 'Round the Mountain	20
Oh My Darling, Clementine	22
Craw Dad Song	24

III. Folk Tales

Today is Monday	28
Viva La Compagnie	30
Sarasponda	32
Polly Wolly Doodle	34
Down by the Station	36

IV. End of the Trail

We Won't Go Home Until Morning	40
Sing Your Way Home	42
Now the Day is Over	44
Taps	46

American Civics
Part I

Patriotic

The Pledge of Allegiance

The Pledge of Allegiance is not a song, but verse. Verse is writing arranged with a rhythm, and is similar to a song. America's Pledge of Allegiance should be understood and put to memory by its citizens, who solemnly promise to be loyal and to defend the American republic. It was originally written in 1885 by Captain George Balch, a Union officer during the Civil War. In 1892, Francis Bellamy revised it. In 1942, Congress adopted the Pledge. In 1954, when the atheist Communist countries of the Soviet Union and China threatened the free world, President Eisenhower and Congress added the words "under God" to signify America's belief in one God.

When the Pledge is recited, citizens should stand facing the flag with the right hand over the heart. When not in uniform men should remove any hat. Persons in uniform or veterans should remain silent, face the flag, and give a military salute.

When saying the Pledge, some think of soldiers who have fought and died for America. Others think of the Founding Fathers and families who sacrificed to create a country that many want to live in. Some think of current soldiers who are in dangerous places across the globe, protecting America from its enemies or adversaries. Some think of their own ancestors, family members, or parents who made great sacrifices to immigrate to America. Whatever a person thinks of, during reciting of the Pledge, all present should be respectful, as the Pledge represents the United States of America, its form of government, all of the Americans of the past and present, and gives honor to those who worked hard to create and defend it.

Important Words to Understand:
1. Pledge means to promise.
2. Allegiance means loyalty.
3. Republic is a form of government where free citizens vote for leaders who make laws.
4. Indivisible means that the country cannot be separated.
5. Liberty means individual rights of citizens, such as the right to vote.

*I pledge allegiance to the Flag
of the United States of America,
and to the Republic for which it stands,
one Nation under God,
indivisible, with liberty and justice for all.*

Betsy Ross

Betsy Ross (1752-1836) made a living sewing flags and may have sewn the American flag.

The Star-Spangled Banner
America's National Anthem
By Francis Scott Key, 1814

During the War of 1812, Attorney Francis Scott Key went to the British to negotiate release of an American prisoner of war. Because he overheard the British making battle plans, he was not allowed back to the Americans until the battle was over. That night and early next morning, he was held in Fort McHenry. From his window he could see the American flag, otherwise known as the Star-Spangled Banner. Inspired, he wrote the following music and later set it to music from a popular sone. The original song has four verses, but normally only the first one is sung.

```
G                                    D
O say can you see, by the dawn's early light,
   G        D           G
What so proudly we hail'd at the twilight's last gleaming,
G                                              D
Whose broad stripes and bright stars through the perilous fight
     G         D         G
O'er the ramparts we watch'd were so gallantly streaming?
G                              D
And the rocket's red glare, the bombs bursting in air,
     G        D       G         D
Gave proof through the night that our flag was still there,
G           C          D
O say does that star-spangled banner yet wave
        G      D        G    C   D
O'er the land of the free and the home of the brave?
```

Francis Scott Key

During the War of 1812, Francis Scott Key wrote the poem, "The Star-Spangled Banner." This later became America's National Anthem.

America the Beautiful
By Katharine Lee Bates, 1893

Katharine Lee Bates was an English professor who traversed by wagon and mule all the way up to Pikes Peak in Colorado Springs, Colorado. Upon reaching the top, Bates was overwhelmed by the beauty, she wrote, "All the wonder of America seemed displayed there, with the sea-like expanse." She quickly wrote the first verse there, and later wrote the remaining three. In 1904 it was rewritten. It was later set to music by Samuel Ward. Though most sing only the first verse, all four verses are shown below.

1. O beautiful for spacious skies, (A E)
   For amber waves of grain, (E7 A)
   For purple mountain majesties (A E)
   Above the fruited plain! (B7 E)
   America! America! (A E)
   God shed His grace on thee, (E7 A A7)
   And crown thy good with brotherhood (D A)
   From sea to shining sea. (D E7 A)

2. O beautiful for pilgrim feet
   Whose stern impassioned stress
   A thoroughfare for freedom beat
   Across the wilderness.
   America! America!
   God mend thine ev'ry flaw,
   Confirm thy soul in self-control,
   Thy liberty in law.

3. O beautiful for glory-tale
   Of liberating strife,
   When valiantly for man's avail
   Men lavished precious life.
   America! America!
   May God thy gold refine
   Till all success be nobleness,
   And every gain divine.

4. O beautiful for patriot dream
   That sees beyond the years
   Thine alabaster cities gleam
   Undimmed by human tears.
   America! America!
   God shed His grace on thee,
   And crown thy good with brotherhood
   From sea to shining sea.

Important Geographical Features

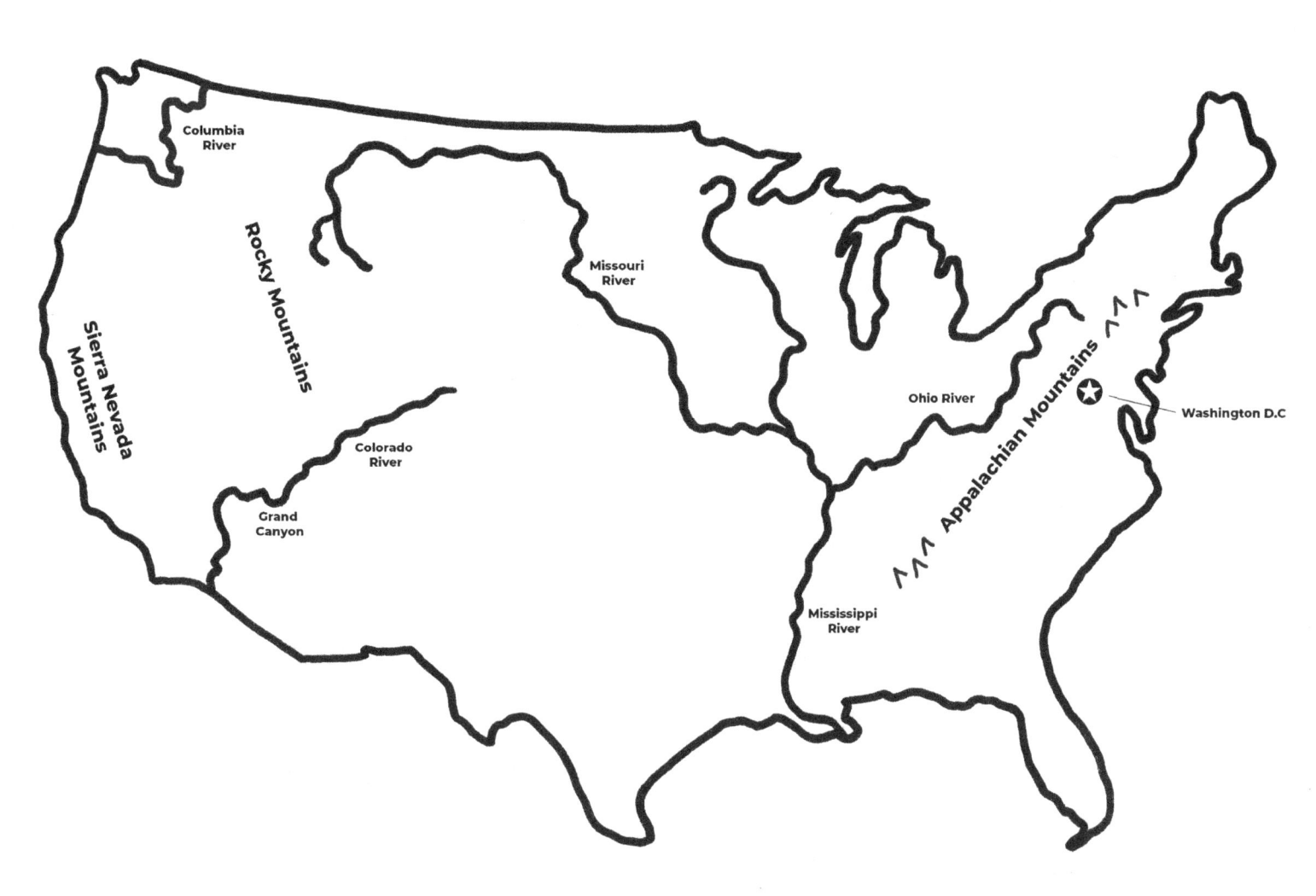

Rivers and mountains fill the United States of America.

YANKEE DOODLE!

Before the American Revolution, a British doctor made fun of the American colonists by writing the initial version of Yankee Doodle. The song meant the Americans were rude, poorly dressed, and conceited. "Yankee" was most likely a nickname of someone named Jan. "Doodle" meant someone who never gets anything done, and "dandy" described someone who dresses in a funny way. As America starting winning the American Revolution, Americans took the song and sang it to the British, showing them that even Yankees can beat the lowly British. Over time, more verses were created for the song that praised the Americans.

```
           G           D          G        D     G          C
1. Yankee Doodle went to town a-riding on a pony; Stuck a feather in his cap and
  D7       G
called it macaroni.
      C                G                     C
Chorus: Yankee Doodle, keep it up, Yankee Doodle Dandy, Mind the music and the step, and
 G     D7   G
with the girls by handy.
```

2. Father and I went down to camp along with Captain Gooding, And there we saw both men and boys as thick as hasty pudding.

Chorus: Yankee Doodle, keep it up, Yankee Doodle Dandy, Mind the music and the step, and with the girls by handy.

3. There was Captain Washington upon a slapping stallion, A-giving orders to his men, There must have been a million.

Chorus: Yankee Doodle, keep it up, Yankee Doodle Dandy, Mind the music and the step, and with the girls by handy.

4. The troopers they would gallop up and fire right in our faces, It scared me almost half to death to see them run such races.

Chorus: Yankee Doodle, keep it up, Yankee Doodle Dandy, Mind the music and the step, and with the girls by handy.

5. Yankee Doodle is the tune Americans delight in, To sing or whistle, dance a jig its just the thing for fighting.

MINUTEMAN

A minuteman was a fighter in the American Revolution who would stop whatever he was doing, grab his gun and ammunition, and be ready to go into battle in a minute.

You're a Grand Old Flag
By George M. Cohan, 1906

George Cohan wrote this song as part of his stage musical, "George Washington, Jr." The title and beginning of the song he received when he was standing next to a veteran of the Civil War who fought at Gettysburg. The veteran had a neatly folded, beaten up flag and said, "She's a grand old rag." Cohan originally wrote the song with the word "rag" but so many complained that he changed it to "flag." This song became the first from a musical to sell over a million copies of sheet music.

Chorus

      F
You're a grand old flag, You're a high-flying flag,
                        C7
And forever in peace may you wave.
                  F
You're the emblem of the land I love,
  G7   C7
The home of the free and the brave.
    F
Ev'ry heart beats true

'Neath the Red, White and Blue,
      D7   G
Where there's never a boast or brag.
       F   C7
But should auld acquaintance be forgot,
  G7   C7   F
Keep your eye on the grand old flag.

The United States Flag

The flag of the United States of America has 13 red and white stripes that symbolize the 13 original states. 50 white stars symbolize the 50 states.

Battle Hymn of the Republic
By Julia Ward Howe, 1861

During the Civil War, Julia Ward Howe heard the Union soldiers singing "John Brown's Body" in Washington, D.C. During the night, the tune stayed with her. She arose from bed and wrote the words for "Battle Hymn of the Republic." The creators of "John Brown's Body" had taken two older songs and put them together, rewriting the lyrics.

           G
1. Mine eyes have seen the glory of the coming of the Lord;
   C   G   D7
He is trampling out the vintage where grapes of wrath are stored;
             G
He hath loosed the fateful lightning of His terrible swift sword:
  C   D7   G
His truth is marching on.

Chorus
 G
Glory, glory, hallelujah!
C   G
Glory, glory, hallelujah!

Glory, glory, hallelujah!
  C   D7   G
His truth is marching on.

2. I have seen Him in the watch-fires of a hundred circling camps;
They have builded Him an altar in the evening dews and damps;
I can read His righteous sentence by the dim and flaring lamps:
His day is marching on.

3. He has sounded forth the trumpet that shall never call retreat;
He is sifting out the hearts of men before His judgement-seat,
Oh, be swift, my soul, to answer Him! Be jubilant, my feet!
Our God is marching on.

4. In the beauty of the lilies Christ was born across the sea,
With a glory in His bosom that transfigures you and me.
As He died to make man holy, let us die to make men free;
While God is marching on.

End of the Civil War

General Lee surrendered to General Grant at Appomattox Courthouse.

American Civics
Part II

Folk

OH! SUSANA
BY STEPHEN FOSTER, 1848

Oh! Susana is one of the most popularly known American folk songs. Some believe Foster combined two other songs into one, and the tune is taken from the "polka," a type of music from Poland. Foster had made about $100 before a publishing firm offered him a royalty of two cents per copy. He agreed, and this made him the first fully professional songwriter in America. The song quickly sold over 100,000 copies, 20 times that of the next most popular song.

1.   (D)   (A7)
    I come from Alabama with a banjo on my knee,
    (D)   (A7)
    I'm going to Louisiana, my true love for to see
    (D)   (A7)
    It rained all night the day I left, the weather it was dry
    (D)   (A7)   (D)
    The sun so hot I froze to death; Susanna, don't you cry.

Chorus
    (G)   (D)   (A7)
Oh, Susanna, Oh don't you cry for me
    (D)
For I come from Alabama
        (A7)   (D)
With my banjo on my knee.

2. I had a dream the other night when everything was still,
    I thought I saw Susanna coming up the hill,
    A buck wheat cake was in her mouth, a tear was in her eye,
    I said I'm coming from the south, Susanna don't you cry.

3. I soon will be in New Orleans and then I'll look around
    And when I find my Susanna, I'll fall upon the ground
    But if I do not find her, this man will surely die
    And when I'm dead and buried, Oh Susanna don't you cry.

A Westerner Playing the Banjo

In the 1800s, many Americans played instruments and sang.

Skip to My Lou
1840s

Skip to my Lou was a dancing game popular during the youth Abraham Lincoln. During the song, a lone boy would stand in the middle of a ring of girls and boys, dancing around the boy. During the words, "Lost my partner, what will I do?" the boys and girls dance around the boy. When the boy grabs the hand of the girl he chooses, that girl's partner then goes into the middle. "Lou" is a Scottish word for "love." There are many versions of this song.

Chorus

D
Lou, Lou skip to my Lou
A
Lou, Lou skip to my Lou
D
Lou, Lou skip to my Lou
A   D
Skip to my Lou my darlin'

1. Fly in the buttermilk, shoo, fly, shoo.

2. Little red wagon, paint it blue.

3. Lost my partner, what will I do?

4. I'll get another one, prettier than you.

5. Cows in the barnyard, moo, cow, moo.

6. Train is a'coming, choo, choo, choo

7. Goin' to Texas, two by two.

Barn Dance!

Americans in the west often had dances in barns where they would sing and dance to "Skip to my Lou."

She'll Be Coming 'Round the Mountain
1800s

This folk song originally was sung to signal the time when Jesus will make his second coming and save Christians. It was later altered to express the excitement villagers had when the stagecoach was coming into town. This song can be sung with hand motions and is a favorite among young children.

                G
1. She'll be coming 'round the mountain when she comes. Toot! Toot!
       G   D
She'll be coming 'round the mountain when she comes. Toot! Toot!
       G   G7   C
She'll be coming 'round the mountain, She'll be coming 'round the mountain,
       G   D   G
She'll be coming 'round the mountain when she comes.

   (Make a hand motion as if you are a trucker blowing his horn)

2. She'll be driving six white horses when she comes (5xs). Whoa Back!

   (Make the motions with both hands as if you are bringing the reins in)

3. Oh, we'll all go out to meet her when she comes (5Xs). Hi There!

   (Make a hand waiving motion with one of your hands.)

4. Oh, we'll have some chicken n' dumplings when she comes (5xs). Yum! Yum!

   (Rub your tummy with one hand in a circle.)

5. Oh, we'll kill the old red rooster when she comes (5xs). Hack! Hack!

   (Make an ax chop to the back of your neck.)

6. Oh She'll wear her red pajamas when she comes (5xs). Scratch! Scratch!

   (Scratch your left shoulder with your right hand.)

7. Oh, she'll have to sleep with grandma when she comes (5xs). Chughh! Chughh!

   (Make a snoring noise).

The Stagecoach

When the stagecoach came into town, people were excited to get letters from friends and family, receive a dress or hat they bought, and to learn of news of the country and world.

Oh My Darling, Clementine

The lyrics to this Western song were written by Percy Montross in 1884, but it is believed the song had existed long before that. It is a story of a young woman, Clementine, who dies drowning during her normal chores. Her lover, a miner, was unable to swim and could not rescue her.

     F
1. In a cavern, in a canyon
             C7
   Excavating for a mine
                  F
   Dwelt a miner forty-niner
       C7   F
   And his daughter, Clementine

Chorus
   F
   Oh my darling, oh my darling
                 C7
   Oh my darling, Clementine
                 F
   You are lost and gone forever
        C7
   Dreadful sorry, Clementine

2. How I loved her, how I loved her
   Though her shoes were number nine
   Herring boxes, without topses
   Sandals were for Clementine

3. Oh my darling, oh my darling
   Oh my darling, Clementine
   You are lost and gone forever
   Dreadful sorrow, Clementine

4. Drove the horses to the water
   Every morning just at nine
   Hit her foot against a splinter
   Fell into the foaming brine

5. Ruby lips above the water
   Blowing bubbles soft and fine
   But alas, I was no swimmer
   So I lost my Clementine

Gold Miner Panning for Gold

In the 1800s, many American men tried to get rich by mining for gold.

Craw Dad Song

This song comes from a combination of Anglo-American play-party tradition and African-American blues. As men worked along the Mississippi River building levees to prevent flooding they sang this along with other songs.

Chorus

F
You get a line and I'll get a pole, Honey
                                        C7
You get a line and I'll get a pole, Babe
F
You get a line and I'll get a pole
Bb   F   C7   F
We'll go down to the crawdad hole Honey, Baby, mine

1. Sitting on the bank 'til my feet get cold, Honey

    Sitting on the bank 'til my feet get cold, Babe

    Sitting on the bank 'til my feet get cold,

    Looking down that crawdad hole,

    Honey, Baby mine.

2. Yonder comes a man with a sack on his back, Honey….

    Packin' all the crawdads he can pack….

3. The man fell down and he broke that sack, Honey….

    See those crawdads backing back….

4. The man fell down and he broke that sack, Honey….

    See those crawdads backing back….

5. I heard the duck say to the drake, Honey….

    There ain't no crawdads in this lake….

CRAWDAD

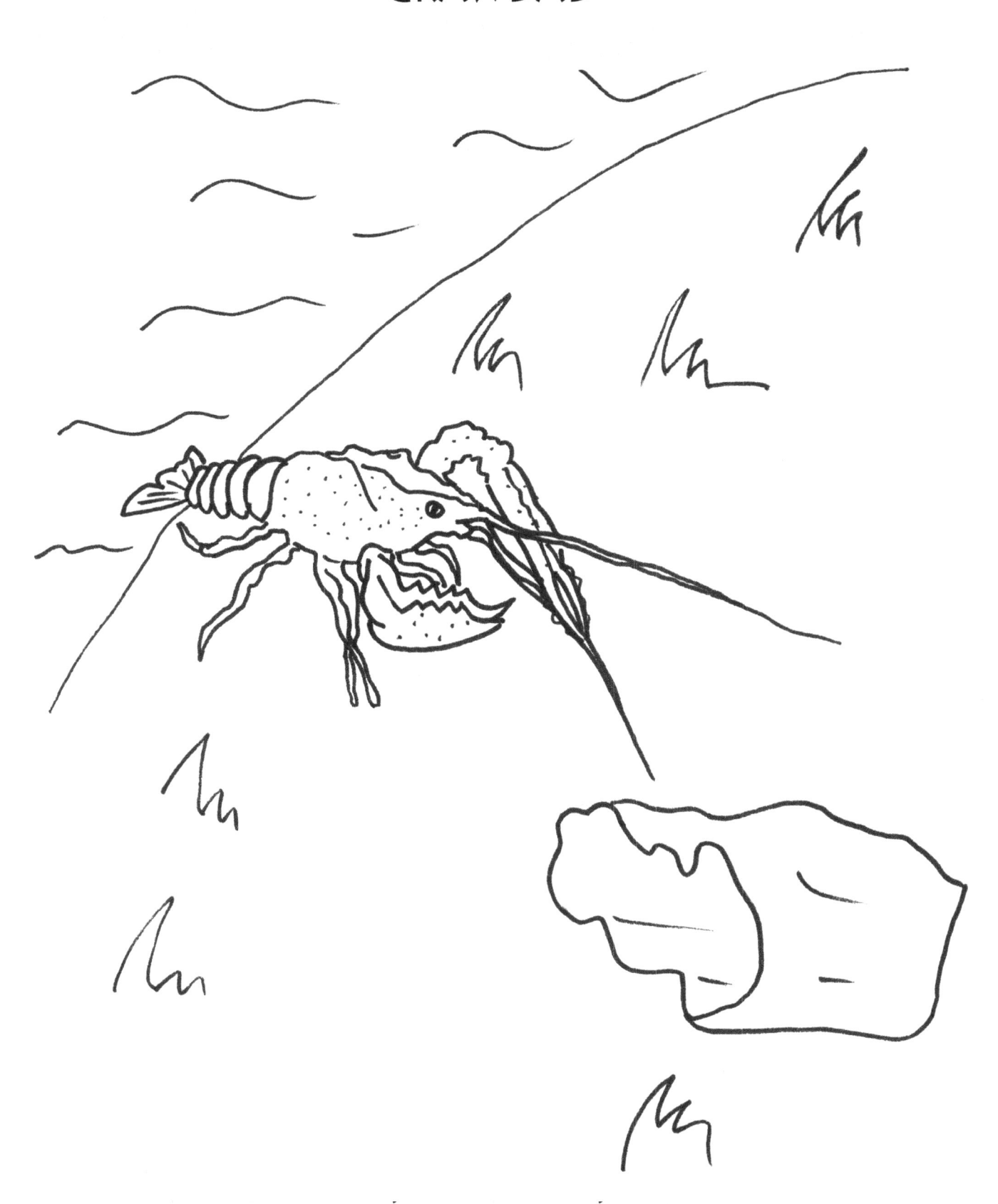

Crawdads are found in the southern states of the United States of America.

American Civics
Part III

Fun

Today is Monday

This child's song is meant to teach the days of the week, but even adults like to sing it!

       D
1. Today is Monday, today is Monday, Monday wash day,
                            A7   D
All you hungry brothers, We wish the same to you.

2. Today is Tuesday, today is Tuesday,
Tuesday string beans, Monday wash day,
All you hungry brothers,
We wish the same to you.

3. Today is Wednesday, today is Wednesday,
Wednesday soup, Tuesday string beans, Monday wash day,
All you hungry brothers,
We wish the same to you.

4. Thursday – roast beef

5. Friday – fish

6. Saturday – pay day

7. Sunday - church

Monday, Wash Day!

This song helped young kids learn the days of the week.

Vive La Compagnie
1818

Believed to be originally an English song meant to teach French pronunciation, it promotes camaraderie, or friendship.

      G   D7   G

1. Let every good fellow now join in the song, Vive la compagnie!

                                            D7   G

Success to each other and pass it along, Vive la compagnie!

Chorus

   G   C

Vive la, vive la, vive l'amour,

  D7   G

Vive l'a, vive la, vive l'amour,

  Em   Am

Vive l'a, vive l'a, vive l'amour

  D7   G

Vive la compagnie!

2. A friend on the left and a friend on the right,

Vive la compagnie!

In one and good fellowship let us unite,

Vive la compagnie!

Friends

Having good friends is one of the greatest treasures in life.

SARASPONDA

The origin of this folk song is not completely known. Some think the Dutch used it to teach young girls how to spin a spinning wheel.

C
Boom da, Boom da, Boom da, Boom da, Boom da Boom da Boom da Boom da

            G7   **C**
Sa ra spon da, Sa ra spon da, Sa ra spon da, Sa ra spon da, Ret set set!

            G7   **C**
Sa ra spon da, Sa ra spon da, Sa ra spon da, Retsetset!

  F **C** **F**   **C**
Ah do ray oh! Ah do ray boom day oh!

G7   **C** **G7**   **C**
Ah do ray boom day ret set set! Aw say paw say oh!

A Spinning Song

This nonsensical but fun song was sung at campfires and at the spinning wheel.

Polly Wolly Doodle
1800s

This children's song first appeared in the 1800s, and it was possibly created by Dan Emmett.

      F
1. Oh, I went down South for to see my Sal
                            C7
   Sing Polly Wolly Doodle all the day

   My Sal she is a spunky gal
                          F
   Sing Polly Wolly Doodle all the day

Chorus
   F
   Fare thee well, fare thee well
                     C7
   Fare thee well my fairy fay
   C7
   For I'm goin' to Louisiana for to see my Susi-anna
   C7   F
   Sing Polly Wolly Doodle all the day

2. Oh, my Sal she is a maiden fair….

   With curly eyes and laughing hair….

3. Behind the barn, down on my knees…

   I thought I heard a chicken sneeze…

4. He sneezed so hard with the whooping cough…

   He sneezed his head and tail right off…

5. Oh, a grasshopper sitting on a railroad track….

   Just picking his teeth with a carpet tack….

6. Oh, I went to bed but it wasn't any use….

   My feet stuck out like a chicken roost….

A Silly Song About Polly!

Westerners loved to sing songs about their girl with fun rhymes.

Down by the Station

This song was first seen in 1931 and most likely existed before then. The tune is exactly the same as the French-Canadian song "Alouette" and "The Itsy-Bitsy Spider." The song is about a railroad engine driver starting the steam locomotive off to work. Pufferbelly means steam engine.

    D   A7   D

Down by the station, Early in the morning,

    D   A7   D

See the little pufferbellies All in a row,

    D   A7   D

See the engine driver Pull the little handle,

    D   A7   D

Chugg, Chugg, Toot, Toot, Off we go!

Puffer Bellies

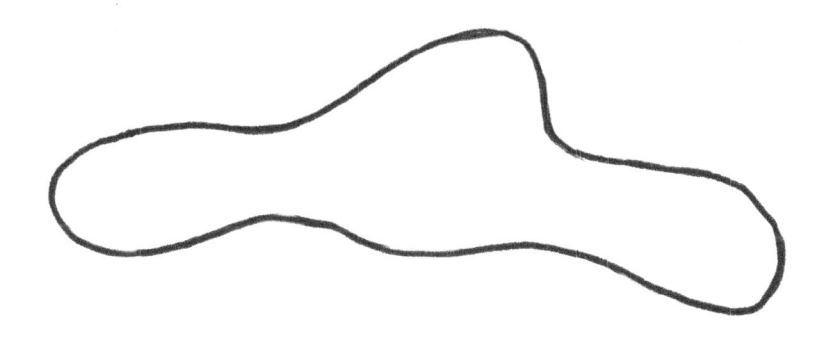

**A puffer belly is an old slang name for a steam locomotive.
Steam locomotives were used to power trains in the 1800s and 1900s.**

AMERICAN CIVICS
PART III

END OF THE TRAIL

We Won't Go Home Until Morning
1842

One of the first times this song was written was in 1842, by William Clifton. It is set to polka music, a traditional Polish dance tune. There are verses to the song, but the most well-known is the chorus. It is sung to the same tune as "For he's a jolly good fellow."

    D   G D   A7   D
We won't go home until morning, We won't go home until morning,
           G   A7   D
We won't go home till morning, Till day light does appear,
 A7   D   G   D
Till daylight does appear, Till daylight does appear,
          G D   A7   D
We won't go home until morning, We won't go home until morning,
           G   A7   D
We won't go home until morning, Till daylight does appear.

THE CAMPFIRE

This song captures the spirit of friends staying up late at night having a good time together.

Sing Your Way Home

Antonin Dvorak and William Arms Fisher, 1922

In the late 1800s, Czech composer was director of the National Conservatory of Music in New York. Dvorak's school was open to men and women and people of all ethnicities, which was unusual for that time. He believed that the United States was uniquely positioned to create a new musical style and thought that the African American songs held the most promise to create new songs. Dvorak wrote the music to Sing Your Way Home, and later, one of his students, William Arms Fisher, wrote the lyrics.

D   A7
Sing your way home at the close of the day,
          D
Sing your way home, drive the shadows away,
         G
Smile every mile, for wherever you roam,
     D
It will brighten your road,
     A7
It will lighten your load,
     D
If you sing your way home.

Sing-Along!

Families that sing together have more fun together.

Now the Day is Over
Sabine Baring-Gould, 1865

Sabine Baring-Gould was an Anglican priest from Devon, England. Aside from being a priest, he wrote novels, folk songs, hymns, biographies of saints, and was a scholar of history. Now the Day is Over is a hymn, a religious song or poem in praise of God. The original has five verses, but it is often just sung with one verse. "Now the Day is Over" is a nice an introduction to the following song, "Taps."

```
    G      D7   G    Em     B7     Em
Now the day is over, Night is drawing nigh,
    A7         G    D7             G
Shadows of the evening steal across the sky.
```

A Going to Bed Song

This song, when sung right before Taps, is a great one to sing right before going to bed, especially when camping.

Taps

Daniel Butterfield, 1862

Union Army Brigadier General Daniel Butterfield, a Medal of Honor recipient, arranged this bugle call as a variation from an earlier one used to signal "lights out" at night. Butterfield wrote "Taps" to replace the firing of three volleys at the end of burials during battle, and it became the bugle call for all military burials. It is also the bugle call to signify "lights out" at American military bases. As it was written for the bugle, it is not officially a song, but a bugle call. Later, however, it is believed Horace Lorenzo Trim wrote words to accompany the song. There are five verses but it is very commonly sung with only one verse. Played right after the "Now the day is over," "Taps" is a fitting way to close the day when camping with children or in a larger group.

G   D7   G D7
Day is done, gone the sun

D7   G   D7   G D7
From the lake, from the hills, from the sky;

     G   D7   G D7 G
All is well, safely rest, God is nigh.

Taps

Taps is the name of the song that is played at the funeral of a soldier, and it is also the song that is played to let soldiers or campers know it is time to go to bed.

Made in the USA
Columbia, SC
07 February 2025